DRAW NEAR T(

Thirty Contemporary Hymns for Worship,
mainly for the Pastoral Services

TIMOTHY DUDLEY-SMITH

music editor:

WILLIAM LLEWELLYN

CANTERBURY PRESS

Norwich

Published in the UK in 2010 by the Canterbury Press Norwich,
St Mary's Works, St Mary's Plain, Norwich NR3 3BH
Website: www.scm-canterburypress.co.uk

ISBN 978-1-84825-022-2

Also by the same author and available from Canterbury Press:
Beneath a Travelling Star: thirty contemporary carols and hymns for Christmas
A Calendar of Praise: thirty contemporary hymns for seasons of the Christian year
High Days and Holy Days: thirty contemporary hymns for annual occasions
in the life of the local church
The Voice of Faith: thirty contemporary hymns for Saints' Days
or based on the liturgy
Above Every Name: thirty contemporary hymns in praise of Christ

Cover design by Leigh Hurlock
Music Engraving by William Llewellyn, Devon, UK
Typesetting by Regent Typesetting, London
Printed in England by Barnwell Print Ltd

Contents

Where, throughout the collection, suggested alternative tunes contain a cross-reference, the letters *CP* signify *Common Praise*, SCM-Canterbury Press, 2000.

1 Draw near to God in humble adoration

BUCKFAST 11 10 11 10 i John S Yolland *b.* 1921

1. Draw near to God in hum-ble a - dor-a - tion, glimps - es of glo - ry lift your heart a - bove: praise him for Christ, the Auth-or of sal - va - tion, one with the Spi - rit in the Fa - ther's love.

OLIVE 11 10 11 10 ii Jonathan Amysson *b.* 1956

1. Draw near to God in humble a-do-ra-tion, glimps-es of glo - ry

An extended version of this setting, with descant, is obtainable from Amemptos Music.

DRAW NEAR to God in humble adoration,
  glimpses of glory lift your heart above:
praise him for Christ, the Author of salvation,
  one with the Spirit in the Father's love.

2   Call on his Name when troubled thoughts are thronging,
      bring him your burdens, cast on him your care:
    he who has made you knows your every longing;
      silent or spoken, God will answer prayer.

3   Open to him your secret sins and sorrows,
      trust in his promise, in his presence rest:
    place in his hands your life's unknown tomorrows,
      whose will is perfect and whose way is best.

4   Render to God the homage of thanksgiving,
      weigh well your blessings, let your song be praise:
    he who gives birth and breath to all things living,
      he will uphold you to the end of days.

Alternative tune: HIGHWOOD (*CP* 28)

2 To God Most High be given
the sacrifice of praise

MORPETH 76 76 D

Cyril V Taylor 1907-1991

1. To God Most High be gi - ven the sa - cri - fice of praise,

the songs of earth and hea - ven, the ser - vice of our days.

Our se - cret sins con - fess - ing in pen - i - tence and shame,

we find a Fa-ther's bless - ing through our Re-deem-er's Name.

TO GOD Most High be given
  the sacrifice of praise,
the songs of earth and heaven,
  the service of our days.
Our secret sins confessing
  in penitence and shame,
we find a Father's blessing
  through our Redeemer's Name.

2   With open hearts, believing,
  with mind and conscience stirred,
the truth of God receiving,
  we hear his holy word.
For neighbour, church and nation,
  a world of human need,
in common supplication
  we join to intercede.

3   May God the Spirit guide us,
  his presence here be known;
our Saviour stand beside us
  to make our prayers his own.
With thankfulness unmeasured
  his mercies we recall,
by Love beloved and treasured
  who loved and made us all.

Alternative tune: MORNING LIGHT (No. 17 in this collection)

3 Christ bids us break the bread

i

KILMORE SM

John Crothers *b.*1948

1. Christ bids us break the bread____ and share the cup he gave,____

in to-ken of the blood he shed for those he died to save.

3i Music: © John Crothers, 15 rue Maurice Hartmann, 92130 Issy-les-Moulineaux, France

ii

FRANCONIA SM

W H Havergal (1793-1870), adapted from a tune in
König's *Harmonischer Liederschatz* (1738)

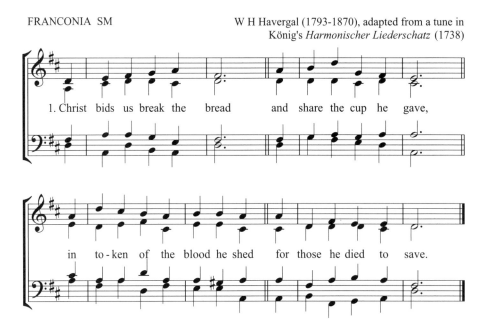

1. Christ bids us break the bread and share the cup he gave,

in to-ken of the blood he shed for those he died to save.

CHRIST bids us break the bread
  and share the cup he gave,
in token of the blood he shed
  for those he died to save.

2 It was for us he came,
    to bear, by human birth,
  a crown of thorn, a cross of shame,
    for every child of earth.

3 The Saviour crucified
    in glory rose again:
  we here remember him who died,
    ascended now to reign.

4 Our hearts his word obey,
    in thankfulness and love:
  we feed on Christ by faith today
    and feast with him above.

5 O Christ, once lifted up
    that we might be forgiven,
  we take the bread and drink the cup
    and share the life of heaven.

Alternative tune: CARLISLE (*CP* 248)

4 We come as guests invited

SALLEY GARDENS 76 76 D

Irish traditional melody
arranged William Llewellyn *b.*1925

1. We come as guests invited when Jesus bids us dine, his friends on earth united to share the bread and wine; the bread of life is broken, the wine is freely poured for us, in solemn token of Christ our dying Lord.

WE COME as guests invited
     when Jesus bids us dine,
his friends on earth united
     to share the bread and wine;
the bread of life is broken,
     the wine is freely poured
for us, in solemn token
     of Christ our dying Lord.

2   We eat and drink, receiving
          from Christ the grace we need,
     and in our hearts believing
          on him by faith we feed;
     with wonder and thanksgiving
          for love that knows no end,
     we find in Jesus living
          our ever-present friend.

3   One bread is ours for sharing,
          one single fruitful vine,
     our fellowship declaring
          renewed in bread and wine:
     renewed, sustained and given
          by token, sign and word,
     the pledge and seal of heaven,
          the love of Christ our Lord.

Alternative tune: PASSION CHORALE (*CP* 119)

5 Father, now behold us

i

PASTOR PASTORUM 65 65

from Friedrich Silcher 1789-1860

1. Fa - ther, now be - hold__ us__ and this child, we pray:

in your love en - fold__ us, wash our sins a - way.

ii

CASWALL 65 65

Melody by Friedrich Filitz 1804-1876

1. Fa - ther, now be - hold__ us and this child, we pray:

in your love en - fold__ us, wash our sins a - way.

FATHER, now behold us
    and this child, we pray:
in your love enfold us,
    wash our sins away.

2   Christ's eternal blessing
      for this life we claim:
faith, by ours, professing;
      signed in Jesus' Name.

3   By the Spirit tended,
      childhood grow to youth;
from all ill defended,
      full of grace and truth.

4   God of all creation,
      stoop from heaven's throne,
and by Christ's salvation
      make this child your own!

Alternative tune: GLENFINLAS (*CP* 303)

6 Lord Jesus, born a tiny child

AQUA SALVA 88 88 88

Malcolm Archer *b.*1952

1. Lord Jesus, born a tiny child and held in Mary's fond embrace, who gravely looked at her, and smiled to see the joy upon her face, look with the same delight, we pray, upon this child we bring to-day.

LORD JESUS, born a tiny child
　　and held in Mary's fond embrace,
who gravely looked at her, and smiled
　　to see the joy upon her face,
　　　　look with the same delight, we pray,
　　　　upon this child we bring today.

2　Lord Jesus, when the children came
　　　　your arms were wide to welcome all,
　　and for this child we ask the same,
　　　　a heart responsive to your call.
　　　　　　Receive and bless, O Lord, we pray,
　　　　　　this child we here baptize today.

3　Lord Jesus, bearer of our sin,
　　　　who died for us and rose again,
　　to make your children clean within
　　　　and free from every sin and stain,
　　　　　　so may this child be washed, we pray,
　　　　　　whom with your cross we sign today.

4　Lord Jesus, reigning now as King,
　　　　whose subjects serve for love alone,
　　let love enlist the life we bring
　　　　and claim this child to be your own:
　　　　　　in faith baptized, received, forgiven,
　　　　　　to be by grace a child of heaven.

Alternative tune: MELITA (No. 24 in this collection)

7 This child from God above

i

from *Kentucky Harmony* 1816
harmonized William Llewellyn *b.* 1925

GOLDEN HILL SM

1. This child from God a-bove,_____ the Fa - ther's gift di - vine,_____ to this new life of light and love we give his seal and sign;_____

ii

WINDERMERE SM

Arthur Somervell 1863-1937

1. This child from God a - bove, the Fa- ther's gift di - vine,

to this new life of light and love we give his seal and sign;

T HIS child from God above,
the Father's gift divine,
to this new life of light and love
we give his seal and sign;

2 To bear the eternal Name,
to walk the Master's way,
the Father's covenant to claim,
the Spirit's will obey;

3 To take the Saviour's cross,
in faith to hold it fast;
and for it reckon all things loss
as long as life shall last;

4 To tell his truth abroad,
to tread the path he trod,
with all who love and serve the Lord,
the family of God.

8 This cherished child of God's creation

i

SPIRITUS VITAE 98 98

Mary Hammond 1878-1964

1. This cher-ished child of God's cre - a - tion, heir to a world of joy and pain, free - ly in thank-ful de - di -ca - tion, Fa - ther, we bring to you a - gain.

8i Music: © Successor to M J Hammond.

ii

NEW BEGINNINGS 98 98

David A White *b.*1944

Unison

1. This cher-ished child of God's cre - a - tion, heir to a
2. Lord, as of old the child - ren found you, when to your
3. Spi - rit of ho - li - ness, de - scend - ing, grant them to
4. God ev - er One, whose care un - sleep - ing watch - es a -

8ii Music: © Selah Publishing Co.Inc. Used by permission.

THIS cherished child of God's creation,
    heir to a world of joy and pain,
freely in thankful dedication,
    Father, we bring to you again.

2   Lord, as of old the children found you,
        when to your side with joy they pressed,
so may our children gather round you
    and in your loving arms be blessed.

3   Spirit of holiness, descending,
        grant them to grow, as years increase,
closer to Christ and his befriending,
    filled with your love and joy and peace.

4   God ever One, whose care unsleeping
        watches about your children's way,
take now this child within your keeping,
    whom here we dedicate today.

9 Be strong in the Lord

LAUDATE DOMINUM 10 10 11 11

Charles H H Parry 1848-1918

1. Be strong in the Lord in ar-mour of light, with hel-met and sword,_ with shield for the fight; on prayer be de-pend-ent,_ be_ belt-ed and_ shod, in breast-plate re-splen-dent: the ar-mour of God.

Alternative tunes: HANOVER (*CP* 546)
PADERBORN (*CP* 227)

B E STRONG in the Lord
in armour of light,
with helmet and sword,
   with shield for the fight;
on prayer be dependent,
   be belted and shod,
in breastplate resplendent:
   the armour of God.

2   Integrity gird
      you round to impart
the truth of his word
   as truth in your heart;
his righteousness wearing
   as breastplate of mail,
his victory sharing,
   be strong to prevail.

3   With eagerness shod
   stand firm in your place,
or go forth for God
   with news of his grace;
no foe shall disarm you
   nor force you to yield,
no arrow can harm you
   with faith as your shield.

4   Though Satan presume
   to test you and try,
in helmet and plume
   your head shall be high;
beset by temptation
   be true to your Lord,
your helmet salvation
   and Scripture your sword.

5   So wield well your blade,
   rejoice in its powers,
fight on undismayed
   for Jesus is ours!
Then in him victorious
   your armour lay down,
to praise, ever glorious,
   his cross and his crown.

based on Ephesians 6.10–18

10 Christ be my leader by night as by day

i

QUEDLINBURG 10 10 10 10

from a melody in Kittel's *Choralbuch*, 1790
harmonized by William Llewellyn *b*.1925

1. Christ be my lead-er by night as by day; safe through the dark-ness for he is the way. Glad-ly I fol-low, my fu-ture his care, dark-ness is day-light when Je-sus is there.

ii

SLANE 10 10 10 10

Irish Traditional Melody
harmonized by Erik Routley 1917-1982

1. Christ be my lead-er by night as by day; safe through the

dark-ness for he is the way.___ Glad-ly I___ fol-low, my fu-ture his

care,___ dark-ness is day-light when Je-sus is there.

CHRIST be my leader by night as by day;
safe through the darkness for he is the way.
Gladly I follow, my future his care,
darkness is daylight when Jesus is there.

2   Christ be my teacher in age as in youth,
drifting or doubting, for he is the truth.
Grant me to trust him; though shifting as sand,
doubt cannot daunt me; in Jesus I stand.

3   Christ be my Saviour in calm as in strife;
death cannot hold me, for he is the life.
Nor darkness nor doubting nor sin and its stain
can touch my salvation: with Jesus I reign.

11 Christ the eternal Lord

DIADEMATA DSM

George J Elvey 1816-1893

1. Christ the e-ter-nal Lord whose pro-mise here we claim,
whose gifts of grace are free-ly poured on all who name your Name;
with thank-ful-ness and praise we stand be-fore your throne,
in - tent to serve you all our days and make your glo - ry known.

CHRIST the eternal Lord
   whose promise here we claim,
whose gifts of grace are freely poured
   on all who name your Name;
with thankfulness and praise
   we stand before your throne,
intent to serve you all our days
   and make your glory known.

2   Christ the unchanging Word
      to every passing age,
   whose timeless teachings still are heard
      set forth on Scripture's page;
   transform our thought and mind,
      enlighten all who read,
   within your word by faith to find
      the bread of life indeed.

3   Christ the redeeming Son
      who shares our human birth,
   and by his death salvation won
      for every child of earth;
   inspire our hearts, we pray,
      to tell your love abroad,
   that all may honour Christ today
      and follow him as Lord.

4   Christ the unfading light
      of everlasting day,
   our morning star in splendour bright,
      the Life, the Truth, the Way;
   that light of truth you give
      to servants as to friends,
   your way to walk, your life to live,
      till earth's brief journey ends.

5   Christ the ascended King
      exalted high above,
   whose praise unending ages sing,
      whom yet unseen we love;
   when mortal life is past
      your voice from heaven's throne
   shall call your children home at last
      to know as we are known.

12 Christ who called disciples to him

WESTMINSTER ABBEY 87 87 87

Adapted from an anthem by
Henry Purcell c.1659-1695

1. Christ who called dis - ci - ples to him from their nets___ be - side the sea, taught and trained the twelve who knew him by the shores___ of Ga - li - -lee, still he calls us to his ser - vice,

say - ing 'Come   and   fol - low   me.'

CHRIST who called disciples to him
    from their nets beside the sea,
taught and trained the twelve who knew him
    by the shores of Galilee,
        still he calls us to his service,
        saying 'Come and follow me.'

2   Christ whose touch was life and healing,
        sight to blind and strength to lame,
    deed and word alike revealing
        mercy evermore the same,
            still he calls us to his service,
            strong in faith to bear his Name.

3   Christ in whom, for our salvation,
        God's unchanging love is shown,
    risen now in exaltation,
        reigning from the Father's throne,
            still he calls us to his service,
            and to make his gospel known.

4   Christ whose calling knows no ending,
        no reserve and no delays,
    by his Spirit's power defending
        those who follow in his ways,
            we are come to be his servants,
            faithful now and all our days.

Alternative tunes: RHUDDLAN (*CP* 356)
                     REGENT SQUARE (*CP* 502)

13 Freed in Christ from death and sin

i

CAPETOWN 77 75

Friedrich Filitz 1804-1876

1. Freed in Christ from death and sin, slaves no more to self with-in,

let a - bun-dant life be - gin__ at the call of Christ.

ii

VESPER 77 75

John Stainer 1840-1901

1. Freed in Christ from death and sin,__ slaves no more to self with-in,

let a - bun-dant life be - gin__ at the call of Christ.

FREED in Christ from death and sin,
    slaves no more to self within,
let abundant life begin
    at the call of Christ.

2   Out of darkness into light,
    given grace to walk aright,
    strength and courage for the fight,
        turned to follow Christ.

3   In the Spirit's life to grow,
    day by day his fullness know,
    and in fruitful lives to show
        we belong to Christ.

4   Bearers of his Name and sign,
    sharers in his bread and wine,
    one with him in life divine,
        keeping faith with Christ.

5   Praise him for his love outpoured,
    lives renewed and hopes restored;
    praise the everlasting Lord,
        glory be to Christ !

14 We turn to Christ alone

ISHMAEL DSM

Charles J Vincent 1852-1934

Unison

1. We turn to Christ a - lone, the Son of God di - vine,

Harmony

to bow the knee be - fore his throne, to bear his Name and sign;

sign and walk

to bear his Name and sign and walk_____ the nar-row way,

sign and walk

to make his love and glo - ry known, his word and will o - bey.

WE TURN to Christ alone,
    the Son of God divine,
to bow the knee before his throne,
    to bear his Name and sign;
    to bear his Name and sign
      and walk the narrow way,
to make his love and glory known,
      his word and will obey.

2   We turn from self and sin
    in penitence and shame;
we trust, to make us clean within,
    the power of Jesus' Name;
    the power of Jesus' Name,
      whose cross is strong to save,
who gave his life our life to win
      from sin and death and grave.

3   We turn from every wrong,
    from every evil way,
who in the Spirit's strength are strong,
    as children of the day;
    as children of the day
      from dark to light we turn,
disciples who to Christ belong,
      his way of life to learn.

4   We turn to Christ as Lord
    who died and rose again,
as those whose hearts receive his word,
    as subjects of his reign;
    as subjects of his reign,
      who calls his servants friends,
our King of love to life restored,
      whose kingdom never ends.

Alternative tune: DINBYCH

15 We turn to Christ anew

HOLBERRY 66 84 D

Ian Kellam *b.*1933

Con moto (not too slow)

1. We turn to Christ a-new who hear his call to-day, his way to walk, his will pur-sue, his word o-bey. To serve him as our King and of his king-dom learn, from sin and ev-ery e-vil thing

to him we turn.

WE TURN to Christ anew
   who hear his call today,
his way to walk, his will pursue,
   his word obey.
To serve him as our King
   and of his kingdom learn,
from sin and every evil thing
   to him we turn.

2   We trust in Christ to save;
     in him new life begins:
who by his cross a ransom gave
     from all our sins.
Our spirits' strength and stay
     who when all flesh is dust
will keep us in that final day,
     in him we trust.

3   We would be true to him
     till earthly journeys end,
whose love no passing years can dim,
     our changeless friend.
May we who bear his Name
     our faith and love renew,
to follow Christ our single aim,
     and find him true.

Alternative tune: LEONI (*CP* 586)

16 When Jesus taught by Galilee

TALBOT HOUSE (TOC H) 88 88 88

Martin Shaw 1875-1958

1. When Je - sus taught by Ga - li - lee he called dis - ci - ples
to his side, his friends and fol - low -
-ers to be, to spread his gos - pel far and wide:
the word of life we still pro - claim, bap -

Alternative tune: CAREY'S (SURREY; *CP* 412)

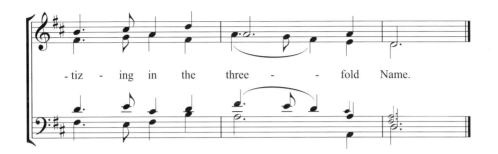

- tiz - ing in the three - - fold Name.

WHEN Jesus taught by Galilee
  he called disciples to his side,
his friends and followers to be,
    to spread his gospel far and wide:
      the word of life we still proclaim,
      baptizing in the threefold Name.

2   That Name declares a Father's love,
      a covenant of grace and care,
    an everlasting home above,
        a family on earth to share,
          beloved and precious in his sight,
          who walk as children of the light.

3   The Name of Christ becomes our own,
        our sovereign Lord and Saviour now,
    to follow him, and him alone,
          whose sign is printed on our brow;
            his service share, his cause defend,
            and so continue to the end.

4   We bear the Holy Spirit's Name,
        who life and truth and power imparts,
    who comes, as once in wind and flame,
          to make his home within our hearts;
            and daily in our lives increase
            his fruit of love, and joy and peace.

5   So in the threefold Name today
        baptized in faith from all our sins,
    we turn to Christ, our Truth and Way,
          the Life in whom our life begins;
            to Christ who saves and sets us free,
            his followers and friends to be.

17 God gives a new beginning

MORNING LIGHT 76 76 D

From a song by
George James Webb 1803-1887

1. God gives a new be - gin - ning to those who hear his call,

who turn from self and sin - ning to Christ as all - in - all:

to know him still more clear - ly their o - ver-arch-ing aim;___

to fol - low him more near - ly, and learn to love his Name.

GOD gives a new beginning
    to those who hear his call,
who turn from self and sinning
    to Christ as all-in-all:
to know him still more clearly
    their over-arching aim;
to follow him more nearly,
    and learn to love his Name.

2   In songs and celebration,
    in penitence and prayer,
we come with adoration
    the bread and wine to share:
to hear his truth expounded,
    before his cross to bend,
and, by his saints surrounded,
    to find in him a friend.

3   May we, his Name confessing,
    unwearied run the race,
and daily seek his blessing,
    his gifts of truth and grace:
his word our souls to nourish,
    his Spirit from above,
whose promised fruit shall flourish
    in joy and peace and love.

Alternative tune: NYLAND

18 O come to me, the Master said

GAINFORD   DCM

Adrian Pallant *b.*1961

Unhurried

Unison

1. O

come to me,   the Mas-ter said,   my   Fa-ther knows your need;___   and

I___ shall be,___   the   Mas-ter said,   your bread of life in - deed.   By

faith in him___   we live and grow___ and share the bro - ken bread,___   and

all   his love and   good - ness   know,___   for so the Mas - ter

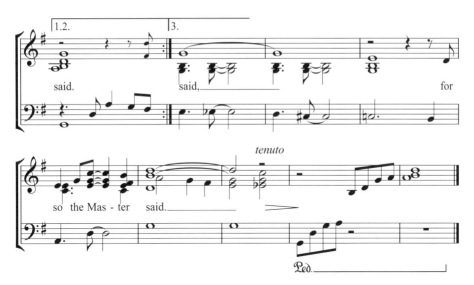

O COME to me, the Master said,
 my Father knows your need;
and I shall be, the Master said,
your bread of life indeed.
    By faith in him we live and grow
    and share the broken bread,
    and all his love and goodness know,
    for so the Master said.

2   Abide in me, the Master said,
    the true and living vine;
    my life shall be, the Master said,
    poured out for you as wine.
        His body to the cross he gave,
        his blood he freely shed,
        who came in love to seek and save,
        for so the Master said.

3   Believe in me, the Master said,
    for I have called you friends,
    and yours shall be, the Master said,
    the life that never ends.
        And so, with sin and sorrow past,
        when death itself is dead,
        the Lord shall raise us up at last,
        for so the Master said.

Alternative tune: COE FEN (*CP* 466)

19 The Lord is here!

i

African-American Melody
arranged Harry T Burleigh (1866-1949)

McKEE CM

1.The Lord is here! His pro-mised word is e-ver- more the same,__ him - self to__ be where two__ or__ three are__ ga - thered in__ his Name.

ii

Melody by C Hutcheson 1792-1860
harmonized by Geoffrey Shaw 1879-1943

STRACATHRO CM

1. The Lord is__ here! His prom - ised word is ev - er- -more__ the same, him - self__ to be__ where two__ or__

three   are   ga - thered   in   his   Name.

THE LORD is here!
His promised word
is evermore the same,
   himself to be
   where two or three
are gathered in his Name.

2   The Lord is here!
Where Christ is come
his Spirit too is there,
   with all who raise
   the song of praise
or breathe the voice of prayer.

3   The Lord is here!
He comes in peace
with blessings from above,
   by pledge and sign
   of bread and wine
to fold us in his love.

4   The Lord is here!
To every soul
this gift of grace be given,
   to walk the way
   of Christ today,
and share the life of heaven.

20 Not for tongues of heaven's angels

BRIDEGROOM 87 87 6

Peter Cutts *b*.1937

1. Not for tongues of heaven's angels, not for wisdom to discern, not for faith that masters mountains, for this better gift we yearn: may___ love be ours,___ O Lord.

NOT FOR TONGUES of heaven's angels,
  not for wisdom to discern,
not for faith that masters mountains,
for this better gift we yearn:
    may love be ours, O Lord.

2   Love is humble, love is gentle,
    love is tender, true and kind;
    love is gracious, ever patient,
    generous of heart and mind:
        may love be ours, O Lord.

3   Never jealous, never selfish,
    love will not rejoice in wrong;
    never boastful nor resentful,
    love believes and suffers long:
        may love be ours, O Lord.

4   In the day this world is fading
    faith and hope will play their part;
    but when Christ is seen in glory
    love shall reign in every heart:
        may love be ours, O Lord.

based on 1 Corinthians 13

21 At Cana's wedding, long ago

STELLA 88 88 88

Melody from H F Hemy's
Easy Hymn Tunes for Catholic Schools (1851)
Harmony by Eric Thiman (1900-1975)

1. At Ca - na's wed - ding, long___ a - go,

they knew___ his pre - sence by___ this sign,

a vir - tue none but Christ___ could show,

to turn___ their wa - ter in - to wine:

and still____ on us his bless - ing be

as in the days____ of Ga - li - lee.

AT CANA'S WEDDING, long ago,
they knew his presence by this sign,
a virtue none but Christ could show,
to turn their water into wine:
　　and still on us his blessing be
　　as in the days of Galilee.

2　What if the way be far to go
and life at times a weary load?
Yet may our hearts within us glow
as theirs on that Emmaus road:
　　the risen Christ become our guest,
　　with him to walk, in him to rest.

3　O Lord of all our life below,
O risen Lord of realms above,
eternal joy be theirs to know,
united in the bond of love:
　　one in the faith, with one accord,
　　one with each other and the Lord.

22 Lord, hear us as we pray

i

From *The Original Sacred Harp,* 1911
harmonized by Willliam Llewellyn *b.* 1925

TEACHER'S FAREWELL SM

1. Lord, hear us as we pray,— a Fa - ther's bless - ing give,— that

Christ be light up - on our way and truth by which to live.—

ii

SANDYS SM

Melody from W. Sandys' *Christmas Carols* (1833)
as harmonized in *The English Hymnal* (1906)

1. Lord, hear us as we pray, a Fa - ther's bless - ing give,

that Christ be light up - on our way and truth by which to live.

L ORD, hear us as we pray,
a Father's blessing give,
that Christ be light upon our way
and truth by which to live.

2   A faith in which to rest,
a living hope, impart;
with charity of spirit blest
in humbleness of heart.

3   The Spirit from above
his gracious gifts increase,
that Christ be all our joy and love
as Christ is all our peace.

Alternative tune: FRANCONIA (*CP* 391)

23 Lord of our lives, our birth and breath

i

CRUCIS VICTORIA CM

Myles Birket Foster 1851-1922

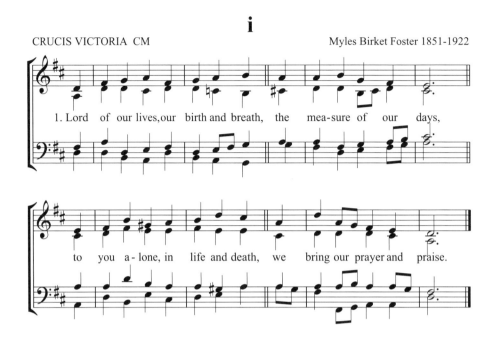

1. Lord of our lives, our birth and breath, the mea-sure of our days,

to you a-lone, in life and death, we bring our prayer and praise.

ii

BELMONT CM

from W Gardiner's *Sacred Melodies,* Vol. I (1812)
Melody probably by William Gardiner (1770-1853)

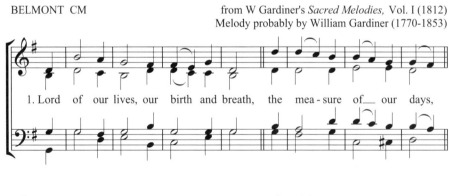

1. Lord of our lives, our birth and breath, the mea - sure of___ our days,

to you a - lone, in life___ and death, we bring our prayer and praise.

L ORD of our lives, our birth and breath,
the measure of our days,
to you alone, in life and death,
we bring our prayer and praise.

2   For love of life and all its powers
by sunlit memory stored,
for tasted joys and timeless hours,
we praise our living Lord.

3   Within the love of Christ we rest
whose cross is strong to save,
by whose eternal hand possessed
we fear not death or grave.

4   So move our hearts, O God above,
by whom all gifts are given,
that one in Christ with those we love
we walk with him to heaven.

Alternative tune: CONTEMPLATION (*CP* 617)

24 Our Father God who gave us birth

MELITA 88 88 88

J B Dykes 1823-1876

1. Our Fa - ther God who gave us birth and ord - ered all our

days on earth, be - neath whose hand we live and move,

the ran-somed child - ren of his love, who gave his Son our

griefs to bear, be near us now and hear our prayer.

OUR FATHER GOD who gave us birth
	and ordered all our days on earth,
beneath whose hand we live and move,
the ransomed children of his love,
		who gave his Son our griefs to bear,
		be near us now and hear our prayer.

2	Though shadows fall, our song be praise
	for fruitful years and sunlit days;
	for surging sea and starry sky
	and hearts where love shall never die;
		for life that conquers death and grave,
		where Christ is risen, strong to save.

3	Beneath his cross our hopes we rest
	where death and life alike are blest,
	and we who move from dust to dust
	in Christ and in his promise trust:
		the Shepherd good, who knows his sheep,
		whose arm has kept them, and will keep.

4	In Christ shall all our hopes prevail,
	no part of all his promise fail;
	for he who here our nature shared
	has won for us a place prepared,
		to live with him that life to come,
		and find his Father's house our home.

25 Lord of the church

LONDONDERRY AIR 11 10 11 10 D

Air from County Derry in the
Petrie Collection of Irish Melody 1903
arranged Michael Fleming 1928-2006

1. Lord of the church, we pray for our re - new - ing:___ Christ o - ver all, our un - di - vid - ed aim.___ Fire of the Spi - rit, burn for our en - du - ing,___ wind of the Spi - rit, fan the liv - ing flame! We turn to Christ a - mid our fear and fail - ing,___ the will that lacks the cour - age to be free,___ the wea - ry la - bours, all but un - a -

-vail - ing,_____ to bring us near - er what a church should be._____

For an alternative harmony arrangement of
this tune, see No. 22 in *High Days and Holy Days*

L ORD of the church, we pray for our renewing:
Christ over all, our undivided aim.
Fire of the Spirit, burn for our enduing,
    wind of the Spirit, fan the living flame!
We turn to Christ amid our fear and failing,
    the will that lacks the courage to be free,
the weary labours, all but unavailing,
    to bring us nearer what a church should be.

2   Lord of the church, we seek a Father's blessing,
       a true repentance and a faith restored,
a swift obedience and a new possessing,
    filled with the Holy Spirit of the Lord!
We turn to Christ from all our restless striving,
    unnumbered voices with a single prayer:
the living water for our souls' reviving,
    in Christ to live, and love and serve and care.

3   Lord of the church, we long for our uniting,
       true to one calling, by one vision stirred;
one cross proclaiming and one creed reciting,
    one in the truth of Jesus and his word.
So lead us on; till toil and trouble ended,
    one church triumphant one new song shall sing,
to praise his glory, risen and ascended,
    Christ over all, the everlasting King!

26 O Spirit of the Sovereign Lord

SENNEN COVE CM

William H Harris 1883-1973

1. O Spirit of the Sov - ereign Lord,
de - scend in power,_____ we pray,
on all who min - is - ter your word____
and teach____ your truth____ to - day.

O SPIRIT of the Sovereign Lord,
    descend in power, we pray,
on all who minister your word
    and teach your truth today.

2   May those whom God has set apart,
        anointed, called and blessed,
    announce good news to every heart
        by want or sin oppressed.

3   Let songs of liberty be sung,
        the lamps of freedom burn;
    as wide the prison gates are flung
        forgotten hopes return.

4   The favour of the Lord proclaim
        in pardon freely given,
    for just and righteous is his Name,
        the God of earth and heaven.

5   May all who mourn, his comfort know;
        their every tear be dried;
    as trees of righteousness to grow
        that God be glorified.

6   O Spirit of the Sovereign Lord,
        descend on us who pray,
    renew your church in deed and word
        to serve your world today.

based on Isaiah 61.1–3

Alternative tune: ST STEPHEN (*CP* 37)

27 Through stormy cloud and darkness deep

RYBURN 88 88 88

Norman Cocker 1889-1953

1. Through storm-y cloud and dark - ness deep, how - e - ver far a -
field they roam, God is the Shep - herd of his sheep
who seeks the lost to bring them home: our long-ing eyes by
faith be-hold one flock, one Shep - herd and one fold.

THROUGH stormy cloud and darkness deep,
   however far afield they roam,
God is the Shepherd of his sheep
  who seeks the lost to bring them home:
    our longing eyes by faith behold
    one flock, one Shepherd and one fold.

2   To seek and save, to guard and keep,
     his own to nurture and defend,
Christ is the Shepherd of his sheep
  who bears us safe to journey's end:
    our dwelling place, through endless days,
    in God's eternal house of praise.

3   What though the path be long and steep,
     and some are faint, or far astray?
Christ gives new shepherds to his sheep
  to tend the flock of God today:
    his word to teach, his church to build,
    and see his purposes fulfilled.

4   Those loving purposes remain,
     more constant than the stars above:
beyond our earthbound sin and pain
  he leads the children of his love
    with joy to stand before his throne,
    and know as we are loved and known.

Alternative tune: ST MATTHIAS (No.8 in *A Calendar of Praise*;
No.12 in *Above Every Name*)

28 Most glorious God, for breath and birth

SAN ROCCO CM

Derek Williams *b.*1945

1. Most glo - rious God, for breath and birth re - ceive our thank - ful prayer, that we, as child - ren born of earth, your life and im - age share.

Optional Interlude between verses

28 Music: © Derek Williams.

ii

Melody from *Scottish Psalter* 1615
Harmony adapted from J Milton, Senior (c.1563-1647)
in Ravenscroft's *Psalmes* 1621

YORK CM

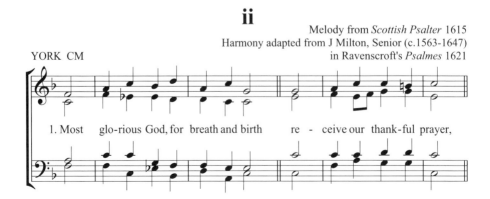

1. Most glo-rious God, for breath and birth re - ceive our thank-ful prayer,

that we, as child-ren born of earth, your life and im-age share.

M OST glorious God, for breath and birth
receive our thankful prayer,
that we, as children born of earth,
    your life and image share.

2   We praise for all your grace imparts,
        the human spirit's powers,
    to sense and know within our hearts
        the love that wakens ours.

3   While in this fallen world we move,
        a world estranged, self-willed,
    our weakness and our frailty prove
        God's purpose unfulfilled.

4   Yet God in Jesus loves and cares,
        and makes his promise known;
    the Wounded Healer feels and shares
        the griefs we call our own.

5   For out of death shall life arise,
        and glory spring from loss,
    when all shall see with wondering eyes
        the triumphs of the cross.

6   As with the dawn the dreamer wakes
        from earthbound sin and pain,
    so resurrection morning breaks
        on Christ's unclouded reign.

Alternative tune: ST SAVIOUR

29 'Set your troubled hearts at rest'

i

HALTON HOLGATE 77 77

Later form of a tune by Dr William Boyce (c.1710-1779)
as given in S S Wesley's *European Psalmist* (1872)

1. 'Set your trou-bled hearts at rest,'_ hear a-gain the word di - vine;_

all our Fa-ther does is best;_ let his peace be yours and mine.

ii

SONG 13   77 77

Melody and bass by Orlando Gibbons (1583-1625)
(rhythm simplified)

1. 'Set your troub-led hearts at rest,' hear a - gain the word di - vine;

all our Fa-ther does is best; let his peace be___ yours and mine.

'SET your troubled hearts at rest,'
    hear again the word divine;
all our Father does is best;
    let his peace be yours and mine.

2   Trusting still in God above,
        set your troubled hearts at rest;
    find within a Father's love
        comfort for a soul distressed.

3   When you come to make request
        know that God will answer prayer;
    set your troubled hearts at rest,
        safe within a Father's care.

4   Be at peace, then, and rejoice,
        loved and comforted and blest;
    hear again the Saviour's voice;
        'Set your troubled hearts at rest.'

from John 14.1, NEB

30 When to our world the Saviour came

i

CHURCH TRIUMPHANT LM   James William Elliott 1833-1915

1. When to our world the Sa-viour came the sick and helpless

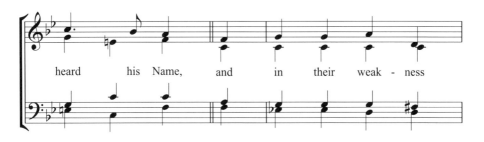

heard his Name, and in their weak - ness

longed to see the heal - ing Christ of Ga - li - lee.

ii

EISENACH LM   Melody by J H Schein (1586-1630)
                                    Harmony adapted from J S Bach (1685-1750)

1. When to our world the Sa-viour came the sick and help - less

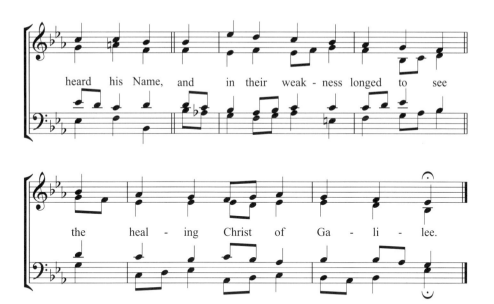

heard his Name, and in their weak - ness longed to see

the heal - ing Christ of Ga - li - lee.

W HEN to our world the Saviour came
the sick and helpless heard his Name,
and in their weakness longed to see
the healing Christ of Galilee.

2   That good physician! Night and day
the people thronged about his way;
and wonder ran from soul to soul,
'The touch of Christ has made us whole!'

3   His praises then were heard and sung
by opened ears and loosened tongue,
while lightened eyes could see and know
the healing Christ of long ago.

4   Of long ago: yet living still,
who died for us on Calvary's hill;
who triumphed over cross and grave,
his healing hands stretched forth to save.

5   His sovereign purpose still remains
who rose in power, and lives and reigns;
till every tongue confess his praise,
the healing Christ of all our days.

INDEX OF TUNES